THE
BIG
BOOK
OF
BIRDS

Words and pictures by
YUVAL ZOMMER

Bird expert
BARBARA TAYLOR

Can you find ...

... exactly the same egg
15 times in this book?
Watch out for imposters.

THE
BIG
BOOK
OF
BIRDS

WHO'S INSIDE?

BIRD FAMILY TREE

How many types of bird are there?

There are nearly 10,000 species of bird and they belong to all sorts of families. Their family group depends on how they look and how they survive in their environment.

Woodland and forest birds ...

... include woodpeckers, toucans, parrots, hummingbirds, peacocks and pigeons

... live in forests

... depend on trees for food, shelter and nesting places

Birds of prey ...

... include hawks, eagles, vultures and falcons

... have great eyesight

... have sharp talons for catching small prey

Owls ...

... usually hunt at night

... have excellent hearing

Perching birds ...

... include sparrows, robins, thrushes, swallows, crows, finches, magpies and white wagtails

... have feet that can grip a perch tightly so they can sleep on a branch without falling off

Seabirds ...

... include puffins, albatrosses, pelicans and cormorants

... have waterproof feathers and webbed feet

... are good at swimming, flying and fishing

Flightless birds ...

... include ostriches, emus, penguins, takahē and kiwis

... have given up flying because they are too heavy, or don't need to fly to survive

Water birds ...

... include ducks, geese, swans, herons, avocets and flamingos

... are good at flying

... nest on the ground

... have webbed feet

I'M A BIRD-WATCHER!

What does a bird think of you?

Wild birds are normally nervous around people. If you want to spot birds outside, you will need to stay quiet and still, and be patient.

Leave no trace

If you're lucky enough to spot a nest, remember that a bird doesn't like its nest or eggs to be touched.

Detective work

A bird will leave clues that it is nearby. It might leave feathers, eggshells, poop or bones from regurgitated food.

8

The call of the wild

You will often hear birds singing and calling to each other. If you learn some common bird calls, it will help you to spot them.

Bird-watching kit

When you are bird-watching, it is useful to take a pair of binoculars. A sketchbook might also come in handy for drawing and taking notes.

9

FEATHERS AND FLYING

Why does a bird have feathers?

A bird is the only animal with feathers. Feathers keep birds warm and waterproof. They are light and a special shape, which helps most birds to fly. Feathers are made from the same material as our hair and nails, called keratin.

Birds of a feather

A big bird such as a swan has up to 25,000 feathers. A little hummingbird may only have 1,000.

Color code

Birds see in color and recognize their own species from the colors and patterns on their feathers.

Glam yet practical

A bird's feathers give it shape, color and pattern. Lots of male birds use their feathers to show off, too. The male Raggiana bird-of-paradise has extra-spectacular feathers that are very long and flowing!

Water off a duck's back

Many water birds, including ducks, produce a special oily liquid that they rub over their feathers to keep them waterproof.

BIRDS ON THE MOVE

Where do birds go in winter?

Nearly half of all birds go on a long journey, called a migration, every year. They normally fly to somewhere warmer and where there is more food to eat. Some fly all the way from the top to the bottom of the world.

Body clock

A bird knows when to start migrating because its body clock tells it to. It knows that when the days get shorter, the winter is coming.

Night flight

Birds often migrate at nighttime when there aren't as many predators around. It is a very dangerous trip. Some birds run out of energy or are killed by bad weather.

Magnetic attraction

A bird finds its way by spotting familiar mountains and rivers along the way. It also looks at where the sun and stars are in the sky. Birds can even sense the magnetic fields in the Earth to work out which way is north.

Down to earth

An emu can't fly, so it migrates by walking or running 300 mi or more.

GREAT GRAY OWLS

What makes a great gray owl so great?

A great gray owl is great in many ways, but it gets its name from being the tallest owl in the world.

Eyes for hearing with

A great gray owl has disks of feathers around its eyes. These act like satellite dishes and direct sound into its ears.

Silent but deadly

As it flies, air passes through an owl's feathers. This means the owls are silent when they swoop down on their prey.

Look behind you

A great gray owl has seven more bones in its neck than a human, which means it can turn its head almost all the way around.

Snow dive

When your dinner lives under the snow, the only way to get it is to crash feet-first through the snow to catch it.

15

FLAMINGOS

Why is a flamingo pink?

A flamingo's favorite food is shrimp and algae. The color inside the food turns the flamingo's feathers pink and red.

Mud soup

A flamingo stirs up mud at the bottom of lakes. It filters the muddy water through its sieve-like beak and eats the tasty scraps of food it finds.

One-legged wonder

A flamingo likes to sleep standing on one leg. No one is sure why!

Strange but cool

When a flamingo gets too hot, it pees on its own legs to cool itself down.

Dance troupe

A flamingo will try to impress a mate by performing a noisy and flamboyant dance routine with up to 50 friends.

17

MAGPIES

Do magpies really steal shiny things?

Magpies do love to pick things up and examine them, but they don't normally steal them. They are also scared of shiny objects!

Magpie parliament

When magpies gather together to find mates, it is called a magpie parliament.

Turn tail

A magpie has a wide, flat tail, which it uses to turn quickly in the air.

Magpies never forget

A magpie can remember people's faces and even impersonate their voices.

His and hers

A male and female magpie have the same color feathers, unlike many other birds. Their black feathers flash green in the sunlight.

KINGFISHERS

How well can a kingfisher fish?

A kingfisher is a brilliant hunter. It uses its sharp beak to spear fish under the water. It also likes to eat water beetles, tadpoles and snails.

Scales and all

A whole fish slides down a kingfisher's throat more easily headfirst. The fish's spiny fins and prickly scales lie flat and don't scratch the kingfisher's throat.

Woah deep, man!

A kingfisher hovers above the water and bobs its head before diving. This helps it work out how deep in the water the fish is.

A filthy habitat

A kingfisher digs itself a home in the riverbank. Its burrow is filled with stinky fish bones and poop!

Can you spot ...

... three female kingfishers? The bottom half of a female's beak is pinky orange.

FLIGHTLESS BIRDS

Why can't some birds fly?

Some birds can survive without flying. Usually they have small wings but their bodies are too heavy to be lifted into the air. An ostrich is seven times too heavy to fly!

Run for your life

A flightless bird will escape danger by running away very fast. An emu can run as fast as 30 mph.

Chill island life

When the takahē bird settled in New Zealand there were no big predators to fly away from, so it stopped needing to fly.

In hiding

A kiwi lives in a hole in the ground in New Zealand. It comes out at night to sniff for worms—a tasty midnight snack. A kākāpō is the only flightless parrot in the world and lives in New Zealand's native forests.

Bit of a weak-wing

A flightless bird has very weak wings, but these can still come in handy. The flightless Galapagos cormorant uses them as a parasol to shade its chicks from the sun.

SECRETARY BIRDS

Does a secretary bird work in an office?

A secretary bird has a head crest of long black feathers that look like old-fashioned feather pens. This is why people call them secretary birds, not because they have day jobs.

Tall and spindly

A secretary bird is the tallest bird of prey at 4 ft.

Squashed snake surprise

A secretary bird loves to eat snakes. When it spots a juicy one, it kills it by stamping on it or pecking at it with its sharp beak.

Bad table manners

A secretary bird usually swallows its food whole.

Glamorous

As well as having 20 striking black feathers on its head, a secretary bird has long, luscious eyelashes.

PARROTS

Can a parrot talk?

Parrots are some of the cleverest birds and can occasionally copy human voices. They do this because they think it is the sound they need to make to stay in touch with their flock.

Turn that frown upside down

A parrot has a top bill that curves downwards and a bottom bill that curves upwards. Parrots like the scarlet macaw look happy all the time!

Home sweet hole

Parrots build nests in tree holes, cliffs and banks, or among rocks on the ground.

Centenarian parrot

A macaw parrot can live for up to 100 years!

What a lovely couple

A lovebird parrot will stay with
its partner for its whole life.

BALD EAGLES

Is a bald eagle really bald?

No! The word "bald" used to mean "white headed" and not "hairless." So a bald eagle isn't thin on top, but white on top!

Eagle-eyed

A bald eagle can see four times better than a person with perfect vision.

A real highflier

A bald eagle's large and powerful wings help it fly to 10,000 ft above the ground—nearly 7 times the height of The Empire State Building!

A talon-ted hunter

For dinner, a bald eagle will use its sharp talons to snatch a fish from a river or a squirrel from the forest floor.

All-American eagle

The bald eagle is only found in North America. It is the national bird of the U.S.

PUFFINS

Why is a puffin called a puffin?

A puffin chick looks like a fluffy puff ball, which is how the bird gets its name. A chick is called a puffling!

Rough edge of the tongue

A puffin has a raspy tongue and spines in its mouth that help it catch wriggly, slippery fish for lunch.

Read my beak

A puffin tells others when it is grumpy by stamping its feet and opening its beak very wide. Sometimes they even wrestle with their beaks.

Flying puff balls

A puffin can fly at 55 mph.

Crash, bang, puffin

Landing is not a puffin's forte.
A puffin often bumps into its friends
when it is trying to land.

31

NESTS

Where is the best place to make a nest?

Wherever it is safe and warm! For some birds that can be in a tree, on the ground or in a cave.

Sew clever

Birds use all sorts of materials to build nests, from sticks and grass to mud and fur. The Asian tailorbird makes a pocket for its nest by sewing two leaves together using spiders' webs for thread.

Shady lair

A cave swiftlet makes its nest out
of spit and sticks it to cave roofs.
People collect the swiftlets' nests
to make bird's nest soup.

Did you know ...

... a cuckoo lays its eggs in other bird's nests?
When the egg hatches, the baby cuckoo is raised
by its foster parents.

Mud hut

A hornero bird makes a hollow ball of mud about
the size of a football and lays its eggs inside.
The mud nest looks like a tiny pizza oven!

EGGS

Why do birds lay pointy eggs?

Pointy eggs fit well inside a bird's body and are less likely to roll out of the nest. A bird lays eggs because carrying a baby in its tummy would make it too heavy to fly.

Big and small

An ostrich lays the biggest egg out of any bird at a whopping 6 in long. A bee hummingbird lays the smallest egg at only 0.2 in long.

Egg sitting

When a bird sits on an egg to keep it warm, this is called incubation. Some birds lose their tummy feathers so that their body heat can get to the egg even more easily.

Colorful eggs

A bird that lays its eggs in a dark hole will have a white egg. A bird that lays its eggs outside will lay a camouflaged egg so that it is hidden from hungry predators.

Cracking gadget

When it's ready to hatch, a baby bird cracks its shell using a horn, called an egg tooth, that is on its beak.

ALBATROSSES

Why is an albatross so big?

From tip to tip a wandering albatross's wings are 11 ft across! Their big wings help them to glide without flapping so that they can save energy on a long trip.

Danger, danger

Many seabirds, including albatrosses, mistake plastic floating in the ocean for food. They often end up feeding it to their chicks too, which can make them very sick.

Cruise control

When it is traveling a long way, an albatross locks its wings in position using a special tendon that holds them out at full stretch.

88 feathers but a chick's got none

An albatross has 88 flight feathers, which is more than any other bird. Some chicks take up to 40 weeks to replace their warm, fluffy, down feathers with their flying feathers.

Island life

An albatross nests with lots of its friends on an island, where it is safe from predators. A female albatross lays her eggs on the island where she was born.

Water, water everywhere

An albatross can drink salty sea water! It gets rid of the salt through a small hole above its eye.

HUMMINGBIRDS

Does a hummingbird hum?

A hummingbird beats its wings so fast that it actually makes a humming sound! It can flap its wings at least 50 times a second.

Did you know ...

... there are over 325 types of hummingbird, each with a different mix of bright, shiny colors.

Five-star flier

A hummingbird is the only bird that can fly backwards.

Food of the gods

A hummingbird's favorite food is sweet flower nectar. It hovers in front of the flowers to feed.

Hungry, hungry hummingbird

To survive, a hummingbird has to eat seven times an hour! That means visiting about 1,000 flowers a day.

PEACOCKS

Why is a peacock such a show-off?

A male peacock has over 200 glamorous, shimmering tail feathers that it shows off in a fan shape. The more impressive the display, the more likely he is to catch the eye of a female peahen.

You'll never meet a ...

... picky peacock. It will eat anything it can get its beak on, including fruit, mice and even baby snakes!

The largest flying bird

A peacock is a very big bird, but it can still fly if it needs to escape from a hungry tiger.

Toe-tally vicious

A peacock has a sharp spike at the back of its foot that it uses to fight off enemies.

Unlucky lady

A peahen has drab brown feathers so that she is camouflaged when sitting on her nest of eggs.

ROBINS

Why does a robin have a red breast?

The European robin puffs up its red chest to warn off other robins nearby. Some birds use their colors to attract a mate, but a robin uses its red chest as a threat.

Fatal attraction

A male robin feeds the female when he is trying to charm her. If he doesn't bring food, she might attack him.

Summer grubbin'

In the summer a robin likes to eat insects, grubs and worms. In the winter it eats more fruit.

Peculiar pad

A robin nests wherever it is cozy. It will lay its eggs in a boot, a plant pot, an old teapot and even in a coat pocket in a shed.

Can you find ...

... an American robin? It is the cousin of the European robin, but it has a black body and its whole tummy is red.

SWANS

Why does a swan have such a long neck?

A swan's long neck helps it reach the juiciest weeds deep under the water. Swans also fish for small frogs and worms.

Can you spot ...

... a North American Trumpeter swan?
It has a black beak instead of an orange one.

Don't come too close!

A swan likes its personal space. If it feels threatened, it will hiss and flap its wings.

44

Wind your neck in

A swan is one of the biggest flying birds. When it is on the ground its neck is a graceful "S" shape. When it is flying, a swan holds its neck out straight.

A swan by any other name

A male swan is a cob and a female is a pen. A baby is called a cygnet.

HOOPOES

How did the hoopoe get its name?

When a hoopoe sings it says "hoo-poo-poo!" and its name is inspired by this special song. A hoopoe sings to others in the area to say "stay off my patch."

An eye for an eye

A male hoopoe is a fierce fighter. It teaches other males a lesson by pecking them in the eye.

Hole sweet home

A hoopoe likes to make its nest in holes it finds in trees or walls. The opening is usually tiny, so other animals can't sneak in.

Crowning glory

The feathers on a hoopoe's head are called a crest or a crown. It fans them out when it is feeling excited and flattens them when it feels calm.

A muddy meal

A hoopoe's beak is the perfect shape for digging. It digs in the soil to find tasty insects but its favorite treat is a frog!

RED-CROWNED CRANES

What is special about a crane?

Cranes are very big, elegant birds. In Asia, they symbolize good luck. They are good at flying and swimming, even though they don't have webbed feet like other swimming birds.

The purr-fect friend

A crane is very sociable and loves to live with friends. It talks to them in a soft purring call.

Stick your neck out

A crane finds a mate by doing a special dance. It leaps into the air, bows, throws twigs and stretches its neck upwards.

Wise weeds

A parent crane will keep its baby safe from owls and wildcats by building a tall platform of weeds under its nest. A moat of water may collect around the nest, like a castle moat.

Bug buffet

A chick hatches out in spring when there are plenty of insects available to eat.

49

BEAKS AND FEEDING

Why does a bird have a beak instead of lips?

Beaks are lighter than teeth which makes it easier for birds to fly. Birds' eggs hatch faster because the baby birds inside the eggs don't need lots of time to grow teeth. Different birds have different-shaped beaks and they all have special uses.

Tear-ific

A hawk has a hooked beak. This helps it to tear its prey into bitesize pieces.

Straight to the point

A bee-eater has a long, thin beak for picking up delicate things to eat. It carefully holds a bee in its beak and taps it against a tree to get rid of the sting before dinner.

What a big mouth

A nightjar's beak is big so that it can scoop up flies as it glides through the air.

Toothy texture

A heron has a sharp beak, like a dagger, which it uses to stab slippery fish.

Nutcracker

A hawfinch has a cone-shaped beak. It is strong and good at cracking seeds and nuts, which are its favorite food.

BIRD CALLS AND SONGS

Why do birds sing?

It can be hard to see where other birds are through thick plants or tall leafy trees, so loud calls and songs help birds stay in touch with family and friends. Calls are short and songs are long and complicated.

A real performer

A sedge warbler sings the longest and most complicated song.

Music makes the heart grow fonder

A pair of crimson-breasted shrikes will sing duets to help strengthen their bond.

Singing lessons

A baby songbird starts learning to sing when it is 10 days old. A baby zebra finch gets lessons from its dad.

The dawn chorus

This is what we call the songs birds sing at sunrise. Skylarks sing first and that's where we get the phrase "up with the lark."

CITY BIRDS

Why do wild birds come to town?

Some birds have adapted to living in cities, near people.
It is warmer there and easier for birds to find food.
Some people even put seeds in their gardens for birds to eat.

Concrete jungle

Peregrine falcons nest on skyscrapers in
New York City. The tall buildings remind them
of the cliffs they live on in the wild.

One man's trash is a little bird's treasure

A city bird will make its nest out of unusual scraps
of trash, from paint pots to shoeboxes.

Cozy commute

A city is often 9°F warmer than the surrounding countryside. Millions of starlings fly into London every night to get a toasty night's sleep.

Sparrow soprano

Sparrows and blackbirds have to sing at a higher pitch to be heard over the loud humming of city life.

30

GIVE GARDEN BIRDS A HOME

How can you give a bird a home in your garden?

Birds always need safe places to live and feed, and if you have a garden or a balcony you can help!

Winter warmers

Make or buy a bird feeder and fill it with nuts and seeds, and some suet balls, to keep your feathered friends fed in the chilly winter months. Make sure the feeders are out of the reach of sneaky squirrels!

Spring delights

In spring and summer, garden birds love to eat insects and worms from the lawn. Don't put out big nuts like peanuts in the spring because little chicks can choke on them.

Birdhouse

Hang a birdhouse on your balcony or from a tree. Blue tits and coal tits like to nest in boxes Robins, wrens and wagtails prefer boxes with a hole in the front so they can see out.

Birdbath

Birdbaths are great for birds who want a drink but also want to splash around to keep their feathers spick and span. Water is especially useful in the hot, dry summer and in winter when their other water sources might be frozen.

Bird-friendly plants

Grow some bird-friendly plants like sunflowers. A sunflower seed is a tasty snack for a hungry bird.

DID YOU FIND...

... the 15 hiding places of the special egg from the beginning of the book?

20-21 Kingfishers

8-9 I'm a bird-watcher!

22-23 Flightless birds

14-15 Great gray owls

24-25 Secretary birds

16-17 Flamingos

32-33 Nests

40-41 Peacocks

42-43 Robins

44-45 Swans

46-47 Hoopoes

48-49 Red-crowned cranes

52-53 Bird calls and songs

54-55 City birds

56-57 Give garden birds a home

BIRD WORDS

Learn to talk like a bird expert

Migration

When a bird migrates, it flies to a warmer country for the winter months. See page 12 to learn more.

Incubation

A bird sits on its eggs to keep them warm so that the chicks develop properly before they hatch out. This is called incubating the egg.

Fledgling

A fledgling is a baby bird that can't fly properly yet because it hasn't grown its flight feathers.

Camouflage

Some birds stay safe by blending in with the background. This is called camouflage.

Carnivore

A carnivore eats other animals.

Herbivore

A herbivore eats plants.

Insectivore

An insectivore only eats creepy crawlies like flies, spiders and beetles.

61

INDEX

To my wonderful niece,
Shir Zommer with love

The Big Book of Birds © 2019 Yuval Zommer

First published in 2019 in the United States of America by
Thames & Hudson Inc., 500 Fifth Avenue, New York, New York 10110

Reprinted 2021

Library of Congress Control Number 2018956165

ISBN 978-0-500-65151-3

Printed and bound in China by Reliance Printing (Shen Zhen) Co., Ltd.

FSC
www.fsc.org
MIX
From responsible
sources
FSC® C102842

Be the first to know about our new releases,
exclusive content and author events by visiting
thamesandhudson.com
thamesandhudsonusa.com
thamesandhudson.com.au